# Unlocking Big Ticket Insurance and Mutual Funds Sales

This book pledges to lead you on a journey toward achieving extraordinary wealth.

Randhir Bhalla

NOTION PRESS

Copyright © <2024> <Randhir Bhalla>



Made with ❤ on the Notion Press Platform

www.notionpress.com

# Dedication

सफ़र में धूप तो होगी जो चल सको तो चलो
सभी हैं भीड़ में तुम भी निकल सको तो चलो

किसी के वास्ते राहें कहां बदलती हैं
तुम अपने आप को ख़ुद ही बदल सको तो चलो

-निदा फ़ाज़ली

This book is lovingly dedicated to the resilient offline insurance sellers who are working tirelessly to adapt and thrive under changing conditions. Their dedication and hard work, despite facing numerous challenges in a rapidly evolving industry, serve as the inspiration for this volume. We acknowledge their efforts to reach new heights in their careers and offer this book as a resource to help them navigate these dynamic times.

# Table of Contents

# Call To Action

**Bonus for early 100 Subscribers**

**1. Get a straight 30% discount if you are one of the first 100 subscribers.**

**2. We will provide free mentoring to the first 100 subscribers for a full year.**

Please book NOW and Register your Name, City, and Email Address by sending a WhatsApp message or mail on following:

**You can connect with Author on**
**Email: randhirbhalla1950@gmail.com**
**Mb: +91 9376117563**
**WhatsApp: +91 9376117563**

# Preface

Dear Readers,

I am thrilled that you have chosen to embark on this journey with this book in your hands. I firmly believe that the time you dedicate to these pages will be immensely rewarding, offering you insights and strategies that could significantly impact your financial future.

This morning, I came across a piece of news that proclaimed, "50 Million High Income Households to be added by 2030 in India" (Source: ET, March 28, 2024). This statistic is not just a number; it represents a burgeoning opportunity for those in the financial sector. The economic landscape of India is evolving rapidly—the rich are getting richer, and the prospects for wealth creation are growing exponentially.

As you absorb this information, a critical question emerges: "Will you be one of these 50 million wealthy individuals by 2030 by selling financial products?" The landscape is set, but the path to personal wealth remains cluttered with challenges and competition.

This book is crafted for those intelligent individuals who are poised to seize this opportunity. The strategies detailed within these pages are designed to position you ideally in the flourishing financial market of India. From understanding how to accumulate wealth to safeguarding it, this guide tackles the fundamental objectives that anyone aiming for financial prosperity must master.

Drawing from over two decades of firsthand experience in marketing financial products, I have compiled straightforward and effective techniques that can help you navigate and succeed in this competitive domain. My conviction in the potential of the financial market is deep-rooted, and I am confident that with the right approach, anyone can attract the right clientele and carve a path to significant wealth.

As you dive into this book, I hope you find it both enlightening and enjoyable. Here's to your journey toward financial success—may this book serve as your compass.


Best wishes,

Randhir Bhalla

# About the Author

Randhir Bhalla & Associates is a distinguished firm comprising Senior Engineers, Chartered Accountants, and Cost and Management Accountant. Among their accomplished team is Randhir Bhalla, an esteemed author known for his expertise in the field. He has authored three notable books:

1. "6 Secrets of Selling 100 Cr (1 Billion) Insurance to HNIs with Ease": In this book, he shares valuable insights and strategies for effectively selling high-value insurance policies to High Net Worth Individuals (HNIs), enabling readers to navigate this market with confidence and achieve remarkable success.

2. "Sell Big Insurance to Unknown Ferrari Owners": his second book focuses on the niche market of providing comprehensive insurance coverage to owners of luxury vehicles like Ferraris, offering unique perspectives and techniques to capture this specialized segment.

3. "How to Make a Million Dollars in the Insurance Business No Matter How Bad the Economy Is": In this book, he shares his wisdom on achieving financial success in any business, even during challenging economic times. Drawing from his extensive experience, he provides practical advice and strategies to help readers generate significant wealth.

Due to his exceptional knowledge and achievements, he has been invited as a speaker at prestigious events organized by esteemed institutions such as FICCI (Federation of Indian Chambers of Commerce & Industry), ASSOCHAM (Associated Chambers of Commerce and Industry of India) in New Delhi, and FKCCI (Federation of Karnataka Chambers of Commerce & Industry) in Bengaluru.

Within India, he has earned a reputation as a leading expert in Financial Business Continuity Planning. His customized Financial Business Continuity Plans have proven to be invaluable assets for business enterprises, their promoters, collaborators, investors, and key personnel within organizations. He firmly upholds the belief that Protection (P) always surpasses Returns (R), emphasizing the importance of robust risk transfer mechanisms. With his distinctive approach, he expertly structures comprehensive Risk Protection plans for HNIs, allowing them to mitigate risks effectively and lead stress-free lives.

# About the book

## A New Era for Insurance Agents

The insurance industry is on the brink of a transformative shift with the IRDA's recent approval of Jeevan Sugam. This new development promises to reshape the landscape, compelling insurance agents to evolve and adapt to maintain their competitive edge.

In the face of growing competition from online insurance platforms, agents must enhance their skills and devise innovative strategies. A key approach will be the customization of insurance products to cater to individual customer needs. Agents will need to offer distinctive features in their products that are not easily replicated by competitors.

Moreover, insurance agents must broaden their horizons by incorporating other financial products like mutual funds, debts, and equity products into their offerings. This diversification, coupled with a continuous enhancement of their knowledge and service quality, will be crucial in meeting the heightened expectations of today's more sophisticated clients.

While the competition may intensify, Jeevan Sugam also opens new doors of opportunity for those ready to embrace change and innovate within their practices.

India is currently in an enviable position, buoyed by a stable government, prudent economic policies, and a youthful demographic, drawing global attention and high expectations.

The momentum seems unstoppable, and the message is unequivocal: overlooking equity investment for at least a decade could be a significant oversight.

For life insurance agents, this is a pivotal moment to diversify their portfolio to include financial products like Mutual Funds before it's too late.

The opportunity presented by this growth is one not to be missed.

This book offers practical solutions and strategies for realizing these ambitions, focusing on financial instruments such as Mutual Funds and Insurance.

Wishing you all the best in harnessing this wave.

# Chapter - 1

# Unlocking Secrets of Big-Ticket Mutual Funds and Insurance Sales.

Before I tell you the secrets of selling High value Mutual Funds/ Insurance you must know the followings:

1. To whom would you like to sell?
2. Why would they buy from you?

The answer to the 1st question is simple. Sell your products to those who have sufficient surplus money to invest.

They will buy from you if you can fulfil their needs/ desires/pain points.

Every human being has 2 basic needs.

1. How to create wealth?
2. How to protect wealth?

Today I am going to show you how you can fulfil their needs/desires and bring about solutions to their pain points.

Before I disclose the secrets of selling High value Mutual Funds/ Insurance with least efforts so that you can become super Rich let me ask you a few questions.

1.  Do you know in May 2014, the Sensex stood at 25,000. Fast forward to April 9, 2024, and it has tripled, reaching 75,000 in just a decade? Industry experts forecast the Sensex to reach 150,000 by 2029.
    Starting on April 3, 1979, the Sensex index reached 75,000 by April 9, 2024, achieving an Internal Rate of Return (IRR) of 16.22%.
2.  India's economic growth has been quite notable over the past decade, highlighted by periods where it achieved the highest GDP growth rates among major global economies. In light of the above what do you think about India's future in next 10 years?
3.  How's your business's top line and the bottom line growing during last 10 years?
4.  Most of the worldwide economies like Japan, UK, Germany is passing through a recession and US is just managing what do you think why India is fastest growing economy?

Let me show you the top market performance during last 10 years.

## BENCHMARK PERFORMANCE

| Year | Nifty | Nifty Midcap 100 | Nifty Smallcap 100 |
|---|---|---|---|
| FY15 | 26.7 | 51.0 | 52.3 |
| FY16 | -8.9 | -1.9 | -13.1 |
| FY17 | 18.5 | 34.9 | 43.0 |
| FY18 | 10.2 | 9.1 | 11.6 |
| FY19 | 14.9 | -2.7 | -14.4 |
| FY20 | -26.0 | -35.9 | -46.1 |
| FY21 | 70.9 | 102.4 | 125.7 |
| FY22 | 18.9 | 25.3 | 28.6 |
| FY23 | -2.2 | 0.3 | -15.2 |
| FY24 | 28.6 | 60.1 | 69.7 |

(Figures in %)

## SENSEX PERFORMANCE IN THE LAST 21 YEARS

| Opening Date | Sensex Points | Closing Date | Sensex Points | Gain/Loss |
|---|---|---|---|---|
| 01-04-2003 | 3081 | 31-03-2004 | 5591 | 81.47% |
| 01-04-2004 | 5741 | 31-03-2005 | 6493 | 13.10% |
| 01-04-2005 | 6605 | 31-03-2006 | 11280 | 70.78% |
| 01-04-2006 | 11564 | 31-03-2007 | 13072 | 13.04% |

| | | | | 25.60% |
|---|---|---|---|---|
| 01-04-2007 | 12455 | 31-03-2008 | 15644 | IRR 38.35% |
| 01-04-2008 | 15627 | 31-03-2009 | 9709 | -37.87% |
| 01-04-2009 | 9902 | 31-03-2010 | 17528 | 77.01% |
| 01-04-2010 | 17693 | 31-03-2011 | 19445 | 9.90% |
| 01-04-2011 | 19420 | 31-03-2012 | 17404 | -10.38% |
| 01-04-2012 | 17478 | 31-03-2013 | 18836 | 7.77% |
| 01-04-2013 | 18865 | 31-03-2014 | 22386 | 8.66% |
| 01-04-2014 | 22446 | 31-03-2015 | 27957 | 24.55% |
| 01-04-2015 | 28260 | 31-03-2016 | 25342 | -10.33% |
| 01-04-2016 | 25270 | 31-03-2017 | 29621 | 17.22% |
| 01-04-2017 | 29910 | 31-03-2018 | 32968 | 10.22% |
| 01-04-2018 | 33255 | 31-03-2019 | 38672 | 16.29% |

| | | | | |
|---|---|---|---|---|
| 01-04-2019 | **38871** | 31-03-2020 | **29468** | -24.19% |
| 01-04-2020 | **28265** | 31-03-2021 | **49509** | 75.16% |
| 01-04-2021 | **50029** | 31-03-2022 | **58568** | 17.07% |
| 01-04-2022 | **59276** | 31-03-2023 | **58991** | -0.48% |
| 01-04-2023 | **59106** | 31-03-2024 | **73904** | 25.03% |
| CAGR | | | | 16.32% |

Between 1st Apr 2003 to 31st Mar 2008, the Sensex rose from 3081 to 15644 (5.07 times) yielded an exponential return with a compound annual growth rate (CAGR) of 38.35%.

Over a longer period of 21 years, the return was decent, averaging 16.32% annually.

Will Indian stock market surpass the above performance in next 10 years?

5. Do you know the power of compounding? Investing Rs. 1 lakh each month at an annual growth rate of 15% will amount to approximately.
Rs. 2.78 crores (27.8 million) in 10 years,
Rs. 6.09 crores (60.9 million) in 15 years,

and Rs. 14.97 crores (Rs. 149.7 million) in 20 years.

6. Are you aware that the long-term capital gain tax on investment in stocks / MF is only 12.5%?
7. Do you know the cost of missing this opportunity?

By posing these questions to your potential clients and informing them about India's growth prospects, you can effectively break the ice and are likely to gain their trust. This approach will make your prospects more inclined to collaborate with you.

## Conclusion:

In conclusion, the trajectory of the Indian stock market and the broader economic landscape present a compelling opportunity for investors looking to grow and protect their wealth. By understanding the historical performance of the Sensex, recognizing the potential for future growth, and leveraging the power of compounding, investors can make informed decisions to optimize their portfolios. Additionally, the relatively low long-term capital gain tax on stocks and mutual funds adds an extra layer of appeal to investing in this market.

As you engage with potential clients, focusing on these aspects not only helps in building trust but also positions you as a knowledgeable advisor attuned to the dynamics of the market. This approach will likely enhance your ability to attract high-value clients and sell premium mutual funds and insurance products effectively. Ultimately, by staying informed and proactive, you can seize the opportunities presented by India's economic growth and help your clients achieve their financial goals.

# Chapter - 2

# Mastering the Art of Cross-Selling: A Real-Life Story of Selling Insurance and Mutual Funds

In this chapter, I'm sharing a real-life story about how I successfully sold a comprehensive insurance and investment package to a potential client. It was the month of March when I received a referral from a prestigious network of High Net Worth Individuals, specifically from a Chartered Accountancy Firm. The referral was for a young, dynamic, and well-educated entrepreneur who had been thriving in the construction business for over ten years. I was informed that he was in search of a suitable term plan -as part of his risk management strategy. The strength of the referral made it relatively straightforward for me to secure a meeting.

Preparation is key in our line of work, so I embarked on a thorough research process about my potential client. I utilized websites, LinkedIn, and insights from my referrer to gather as much relevant information as possible. Given that my referrer is a qualified chartered accountant and also serves as an auditor for the client's company, accessing financial details was more straightforward than usual.

Here's a summary of the preliminary information I gathered about the client:

- Name: Mr. Ramesh Patel

- Age: 40

- Profession: Real Estate Developer

- Company Type: Private Limited

- Share Holding –

Personal – 50%

Wife – 38%

- Secured Loans: Rs. 50 Crores, with 200% collateral plus a personal guarantee provided to the bank

- Annual Sales Revenue: Rs.110 Crores

- Net Profit: Rs.12 Crores

- Annual Growth Rate of Business – 20%

- Current Life Insurance Coverage: Negligible

- Health Insurance: Rs. 5 Lacs

- Investments: Primarily in land and real estate

- Personal Income Tax Return: Rs. 1.2 Crores (Rs. 12.0 million)

- Risk Appetite: High

- Family: A spouse and two young children

- Habits: None noted

- Health Status: Good

Armed with this information, I felt prepared and confident to engage in a meaningful conversation with my prospect.

Stay tuned for the next chapter, where I'll delve into the details of our initial meeting.

# Chapter - 3

# Diversify Beyond Life Insurance: Offer a Range of Financial Products.

## The moment has arrived to offer a full spectrum of financial products.

Throughout your career, you've dedicated yourself to selling life insurance exclusively. However, only a handful have ventured beyond, embracing the challenge of diversifying into other financial products, such as Mutual Funds and Health Insurance. It's becoming increasingly clear that the landscape has shifted. Relying solely on life insurance sales is no longer a viable strategy to meet your financial objectives.

Today's clients are seeking more than just insurance; they're looking for expert guidance on wealth creation, which often tops their list of priorities. In this discussion, I aim to shed light on several key strategies for wealth generation, urging a broader approach to the financial products you offer.

## Essential Steps Towards Wealth Building

While engaging with the prospect, take this chance to inform them about wealth creation. This strategy sets you apart from typical financial product sellers and aids in building trust with the prospect.

Discovering the path to wealth might seem like uncovering a secret spell for becoming incredibly wealthy in one's lifetime. The concept is surprisingly straightforward:

To amass significant wealth, one must:

1. Earn well – Focusing on unique opportunities in the financial industry that set you apart.

2. Save well – Being diligent and disciplined about saving.

3. Invest wisely – Making smart investment choices that grow your wealth

At first glance, this strategy may appear elementary, almost too well-known to be dubbed magical. However, the true mastery lies not in knowing these steps but in executing them effectively. For instance:

- Without sufficient earnings, saving and investing become moot points.

- Ample earnings with no savings offer no foundation for investment.

- Earning and saving without wise investment strategies leads to missed opportunities.

This triad must be enacted concurrently for real success. It's common for younger individuals to resist saving, often preferring to indulge in immediate pleasures rather than secure their financial future. Conversely, some save without leveraging their capital through smart investments, resulting in stagnant or underperforming assets, such as investments that don't even outpace inflation, effectively eroding wealth instead of building it.

The essence of this strategy is a balanced, simultaneous application of earning, saving, and intelligent investing.

# Chapter - 4

# Why Opting Out of Selling Financial Products Could Be a Big Miss

In today's fast-paced economic environment, diversifying revenue streams is not just an advantage—it's a necessity. For professionals and businesses alike, opting out of participating in the sale of financial products could represent a missed opportunity of substantial proportions. Here's why:

## 1. Expanding Market Reach

The financial sector is burgeoning with opportunities, driven by increasing consumer awareness and demand for financial literacy. Engaging in selling financial products opens up a new client base, extending your market reach. Whether you are a financial advisor, a corporate entity, or an entrepreneur, adding financial products to your offerings can attract a broader audience that seeks financial empowerment.

## 2. Increased Revenue Streams

Financial products, ranging from Life / Health Insurance policies to Investment Funds, offer lucrative commission structures and recurring income opportunities. By not participating, you might be sidelining a potentially stable and significant source of revenue that could bolster your financial health, especially in volatile market conditions.

### 3. Strengthened Client Relationships

Offering financial products allows for more comprehensive service to clients. When clients can rely on you for both advice and product solutions, you become an indispensable part of their financial planning. This trust builds stronger, longer-lasting client relationships and enhances client retention rates.

### 4. Staying Competitive

The financial landscape is competitive and ever evolving. Companies and professionals who offer a wide range of services, including financial products, are better positioned to adapt to changes in the market. By staying on the cutting edge of financial trends and products, you demonstrate your commitment to meeting your clients' needs and staying ahead in the game.

### 5. Professional Growth and Development

Learning about and selling financial products enriches your expertise. It keeps you informed about the financial market's dynamics, which is crucial for your professional development. This knowledge not only aids in personal growth but also enhances your credibility and authority in the field, making you a go-to expert.

**Conclusion:**

While the decision to sell financial products is significant, the potential benefits are too substantial to ignore. From enhancing your service offering to increasing revenue, and from fostering client loyalty to ensuring competitive advantage, the role of financial products in business strategy is integral. Ignoring this avenue might not just be a missed opportunity—it could also mean lagging behind in a world where financial acumen is increasingly valued.

Engage with the market, understand the needs, and consider whether participating in the sale of financial products aligns with your strategic goals. The right choice could propel you forward in ways you might not have imagined.

This content aims to highlight the critical advantages of engaging in the sale of financial products and the potential drawbacks of opting out.

# Chapter - 5

# Not Selling Mutual Fund as a Financial Product is a missed opportunity in India.

In India's burgeoning financial landscape, mutual funds have emerged as one of the most dynamic and accessible investment avenues. The Indian mutual fund industry has witnessed exponential growth over the past few years, buoyed by a rising middle class, increased financial literacy, and a favourable regulatory environment. In this context, not offering mutual funds as a part of one's financial product portfolio can be seen as a missed opportunity for financial advisors and institutions.

## The Growth Trajectory of Mutual Funds in India

Mutual funds in India have gained significant traction, thanks to the diversified investment options they offer, catering to various risk appetites and financial goals. The ease of investment through Systematic Investment Plans (SIPs), along with the advantage of professional fund management, has made mutual funds a preferred choice for many investors, from seasoned to novices.

The increase in the number of demat accounts and the surge in equity participation are indicative of a broader acceptance and appetite for investment products, including mutual funds. The Assets Under Management (AUM) of the Indian mutual fund industry have seen a remarkable increase, underscoring the trust and confidence investors place in mutual funds.

## Missed Opportunity for Financial Advisors and Institutions

For financial advisors and institutions, mutual funds offer a versatile tool to meet a wide range of client needs, from wealth creation to tax planning. Not incorporating mutual funds into the financial product mix can lead to a significant gap in serving clients effectively. Here are a few reasons why overlooking mutual funds can be a missed opportunity:

**Diversification:** Mutual funds provide a convenient way to achieve portfolio diversification, reducing risk

and enhancing the potential for returns. Advisors can cater to various client profiles by recommending suitable mutual fund schemes.

**Client Retention:** By offering a comprehensive suite of financial products, including mutual funds, advisors can enhance client retention. Investors prefer a one-stop solution for all their investment needs, and mutual funds can be a key offering.

**Revenue Streams:** Mutual funds offer financial advisors and institutions an additional revenue stream through commission and advisory fees. With the growing investor base and SIP contributions, the potential for revenue generation is significant.

**Market Sentiment:** The positive market sentiment towards mutual funds, driven by regulatory support and market performance, creates an opportune moment to introduce clients to mutual fund investments.

### Forward-Looking Strategies

To capitalize on this opportunity, financial advisors and institutions need to integrate mutual funds into their product offerings actively. This includes educating clients about the benefits of mutual funds, understanding their financial goals, and recommending suitable schemes. Leveraging technology to simplify the investment process and offering personalized advisory services can further enhance the appeal of mutual funds.

In conclusion, as India's financial market matures, mutual funds stand out as a key component of a well-rounded investment portfolio. For financial advisors and institutions, not offering mutual funds is not just a missed opportunity but a disservice to clients seeking comprehensive financial solutions. By embracing mutual funds, financial professionals can better serve their clients, tapping into the growth potential of India's investment landscape.

# Chapter – 6

# You will likely regret missing out on investing in India's financial products in the next decade.

**Growing investments in financial products in India.**

India's financial landscape is undergoing a transformation, marked by a surge in investments across a wide range of financial products. This uptick is not just a testament to the growing economic stability and confidence in the Indian market but also reflects the evolving financial literacy and investment savvy of the Indian populace.

The rise in investments can be attributed to several key factors. First, India's economy has shown resilience and steady growth, supported by stable political governance and forward-looking policies that encourage investment. These conditions have fostered a favourable environment for both domestic and international investors, looking to capitalize on India's growth trajectory.

Second, the digital revolution in India has played a crucial role. The ease of access to financial services, through digital platforms, has demystified investment processes and made financial products more accessible to a broader segment of the population. The introduction of user-friendly apps and platforms has simplified the process of opening demat accounts, trading in stocks, and investing in mutual funds, allowing individuals to manage their finances with just a few clicks.

The mutual fund industry, in particular, has seen unprecedented growth. Systematic Investment Plans (SIPs), a popular way to invest in mutual funds, have seen a significant increase in average monthly contributions over the last year. This growth signifies a shift towards more disciplined and long-term investment strategies among Indian investors.

Additionally, the burgeoning middle class in India, with increasing disposable incomes and a higher propensity to save and invest, has been a key driver of growth in investments. There's a growing awareness about the benefits of investing in a mix of financial products, including equities, mutual funds, and insurance, to achieve financial goals and secure one's financial future.

However, the landscape is not without challenges. Financial literacy remains a barrier for a significant portion of the population, underscoring the need for continued education and outreach to ensure that more individuals can make informed investment decisions.

In conclusion, the growing investments in financial products in India signal a maturing market and a more financially savvy population. With continued economic stability, technological advancements, and efforts to improve financial literacy, India is poised for even greater strides in its financial sector. This trend not only benefits individual investors but also contributes to the broader economic growth and stability of the country.

# Chapter - 7

# Growth in SIPs during last 3 years in India

## Is this trend sustainable?

**In-depth Analysis of SIP Growth in India Over the Last Three Years: Dynamics, Trends, and Forecast**

The last three years have marked a significant phase in the evolution of Systematic Investment Plans (SIPs) in India, showcasing substantial growth and an expanding investor base. This period has not only solidified SIPs' role in personal financial planning but also highlighted the broader shift towards more disciplined investment practices among Indian savers.

Below, we delve deeper into the trends, underlying factors, and the potential future of SIP investments in India.

## Detailed Overview of SIP Growth

Between 2021 and 2024, SIP inflows have demonstrated robust growth, underscoring an increasing trust and preference for systematic investments. For example, the total SIP contributions in fiscal year 2023 escalated to approximately ₹1.56 lakh crore, up by 25.2% from the previous year. This surge continued into 2024, with SIP inflows surpassing ₹20,000 crore in a single month (April), setting a new record for monthly contributions.

Source: Mint, India Today, AMFI India

## Comprehensive Examination of Factors Driving SIP Inflows

### 1. Financial Literacy and Accessibility:

The significant push towards enhancing financial literacy and the democratization of financial services has brought a larger demographic into the investment fold. Government initiatives aimed at digital financial inclusion have facilitated this reach beyond metropolitan areas into Tier II and Tier III cities, thus broadening the investor base significantly.

### 2. Macroeconomic Stability:

India's economic landscape has been favourable, characterized by consistent GDP growth, low to moderate inflation and strengthening job markets. These factors have provided a stable backdrop for regular and long-term investments in mutual funds through SIPs, boosting investor confidence and contributing to the volume of inflows.

## 3. Regulatory Enhancements:

The proactive approach of regulatory bodies like SEBI in implementing investor-friendly policies has significantly influenced SIP growth. Measures such as simplified KYC processes and extensive investor education campaigns have lowered entry barriers and enhanced investor engagement and retention.

## Trends in SIP Allocations and Preferences

The allocation of SIP investments has predominantly favoured equity funds, reflecting a preference for higher returns despite potential risks. This shift towards equity and hybrid funds has been supported by substantial inflows, contrasting with the outflows observed in debt funds during the same period. This trend highlights a broader risk appetite among Indian investors, motivated by the long-term growth potential of the equity market.

## Assessing the Sustainability of SIP Growth

The sustainability of this upward trajectory in SIP inflows is contingent on several factors:

**Market Dynamics:** While SIPs offer a way to mitigate timing risks in volatile markets through dollar-cost averaging, extended periods of market downturns or excessive volatility can still deter potential new investors or prompt current investors to withdraw.

**Economic Indicators:** Ongoing economic stability is crucial for the continuation of SIP growth. Any negative shifts in key economic indicators, such as GDP, inflation, or employment rates, could diminish disposable income and savings, adversely affecting SIP contributions.

**Investor Sentiment:** The sentiment and behaviour of investors towards mutual funds and systematic investing play a critical role. Continued positive engagement depends on the mutual fund industry and regulatory bodies maintaining and enhancing investor confidence through education and transparent practices.

# Chapter - 8

## It's never late to become Financial Advisor in India

When a friend learned about the topic of my upcoming book, he asked me, "Isn't it too late to enter the financial product market? The competition is intense, and it's tough to outperform the established players."

Here's how I responded:

Indeed, it's never too late to become a financial advisor in India, and several statistics and trends support this assertion:

1. **Growing Financial Assets**: India's financial assets have been consistently growing. According to a report by Boston Consultancy Group - an American Global Management Consulting Firm, India's personal

financial wealth is expected to grow from $3 trillion in 2020 to $5 trillion by 2025, representing a compound annual growth rate (CAGR) of approximately 10%. This growth in personal wealth increases the need for financial advisors who can guide investors in managing and growing their assets.

2. **Increasing Investments in Mutual Funds:** The mutual fund industry in India has seen robust growth over the past decade. As per the Association of Mutual Funds in India (AMFI), the assets under management (AUM) of the Indian mutual fund industry have grown from approximately Rs.10 trillion in March 2014 to over Rs.38 trillion by the end of 2022. The AMFI further reported a net AUM of Rs 51,09,071.8 crore at the end of December 2023, reflecting the robustness of the India growth story. December 2023 witnessed an influx of approximately Rs.17,000 crore into equity mutual funds, marking a dynamic shift in investor sentiment.

This upward trajectory suggests a rising demand for financial advice related to mutual funds.

3. **Proliferation of Financial Products:** There has been a significant increase in the variety and complexity of financial products available in the market. Products such as mutual funds, stocks, bonds, ETFs (Exchange-Traded Fund), and newer financial instruments like REITs and InvITs – (REITs and InvITs are investment vehicles that stand for Real Estate Investment Trusts and Infrastructure Investment Trusts, respectively) require specialized

knowledge. The complexity and variety of these products can make the role of a financial advisor critical for investors who may not have the expertise to navigate these options independently.

4. **Digital Penetration:** The digital revolution in India, including widespread internet usage and smartphone penetration, has made financial services more accessible to a broader audience. According to the Internet and Mobile Association of India, internet users in India were expected to reach over 900 million by the end of 2025. This digital connectivity allows financial advisors to reach and service clients across geographies, reducing barriers to entry in the advisory field.

5. **Demographic Factors:** With a large and relatively young population, India presents a significant opportunity for long-term financial planning. The median age in India is around 28 years, which is ideal for financial planning services that focus on long-term investments and retirement planning.

6. **Regulatory Framework and Education:** The Securities and Exchange Board of India (SEBI) has improved regulations around financial advisors to protect consumers and enhance the quality of advice, through certifications and continuing education requirements. This ensures that new entrants can be trained to a high standard, providing confidence both to them and their clients.

These statistics and trends highlight that there is substantial and growing demand for financial advisory services in India, making it a viable career option regardless of when one chooses to enter the field. The ongoing need for financial education and guidance combined with a growing and diversifying financial market makes becoming a financial advisor a promising opportunity.

In conclusion, entering the field of financial advisory in India presents a timely and promising opportunity. The convergence of India's rapidly expanding personal financial wealth, the robust growth of the mutual fund industry, and the increasing complexity of financial products all signal a rising demand for expert financial guidance. Coupled with technological advancements that facilitate greater reach and efficiency, and a regulatory environment that ensures professionalism and trust, the prospects for financial advisors look increasingly bright. Moreover, with a youthful demographic poised to invest for long-term gains, the need for skilled advisors is more relevant than ever. Therefore, for those considering a career as a financial advisor in India, the market conditions and trends suggest that it is indeed never too late to start.

# Chapter – 9

## First thing First.

## What a Financial Advisor should know?

**Dos and don'ts while suggesting investment in Financial products.**

When investing in financial products, it's crucial to follow certain dos and don'ts to ensure that your investments are safe, strategic, and aligned with your financial goals. Here's a guide to some essential practices to adopt and pitfalls to avoid:

**Dos:**

1. **Do Your Homework:** Research thoroughly before investing in any financial product. Understand the product's features, risks, and potential returns. Familiarize yourself with the terms and conditions associated with the investment.

2. **Diversify Your Portfolio:** Spread your investments across different asset classes (stocks, bonds, mutual funds, etc.) to mitigate risk. Diversification can help protect your portfolio from volatility in any single asset class.

3. **Set Clear Financial Goals:** Identify your financial goals, such as retirement, buying a home, or

funding education. Tailor your investment choices to align with these objectives and your risk tolerance.

4. **Consider the Time Horizon:** Match your investments with your time horizon. If you have long-term goals, you may opt for equity or mutual funds that typically offer higher returns over a longer period. For short-term goals, consider safer investments like fixed deposits or debt funds.

5. **Review and Rebalance Regularly:** Regularly review your investment portfolio to ensure it stays aligned with your financial goals. Rebalance it as necessary, especially in response to significant life events or changes in financial circumstances.

6. **Seek Professional Advice:** If unsure, consult with a financial advisor. A professional can provide personalized advice based on your financial situation and goals.

**Don'ts:**

1. **Don't Invest Based on Emotions:** Avoid making investment decisions based solely on emotions or market hype. Emotional investing can lead to poor decision-making and timing errors.

2. **Don't Chase Past Performance:** Just because a product performed well in the past doesn't guarantee future returns. Assess each investment on its current merits and future potential.

3. **Don't Ignore Fees:** Be aware of any fees or charges associated with your investment. High fees can significantly erode returns over time, especially in managed funds like mutual funds.

4. **Don't Overlook Tax Implications:** Understand the tax implications of your investments. Some financial products offer tax benefits which can enhance overall returns, while others may incur higher tax liabilities.

5. **Don't Put All Your Eggs in One Basket:** Avoid investing all your money in a single asset class or product. Over-concentration increases risk and limits potential returns from other types of investments.

6. **Don't Ignore Economic and Market Trends:** Stay informed about broader economic and market trends that could impact your investments. Changes in interest rates, inflation, political stability, and global events can influence market performance.

## Conclusion:

By adhering to these Dos and Don'ts, you can make more informed and effective investment decisions, helping you achieve your financial objectives while managing risk effectively.

# Chapter - 10

# Educate your prospects about the secrets to successful investing.

## Investment is all about balancing Risk v/s Returns.

Investment is a fundamental component of financial planning that involves the careful allocation of resources with the aim of generating future returns. At the heart of investment strategy lies the principle of balancing risk versus returns, a concept that requires investors to navigate the delicate interplay between the potential for high rewards and the likelihood of incurring losses.

## Understanding Risk and Returns

**Risk** refers to the possibility that an investment's actual returns will differ from the expected returns and may result in the loss of some or all of the original investment. Different types of investments carry varying levels of risk, influenced by factors such as market volatility, economic conditions, and the financial health of the investment vehicle.

**Returns**, on the other hand, represent the gain or income generated from an investment over a period of time. Returns can come in the form of interest, dividends, or capital appreciation, and they are the primary goal for most investors.

**The Risk-Return Trade-Off**

The risk-return trade-off is a fundamental principle in investing that suggests that the potential return on an investment is directly correlated with the level of risk associated with it. High-risk investments typically offer the potential for higher returns as a compensation for the increased uncertainty and higher chance of loss. Conversely, low-risk investments usually provide lower returns, reflecting their lower volatility and greater predictability.

**Strategies for Balancing Risk and Returns**

1. **Diversification:** Spreading investments across different asset classes (such as stocks, bonds, and real estate) can reduce risk without proportionately lowering returns. Diversification helps mitigate the impact of poor performance in any single investment.

2. **Asset Allocation:** Tailoring the mix of assets in a portfolio based on an individual's risk tolerance, investment goals, and time horizon can optimize the balance between risk and returns. Younger investors might lean towards higher-risk, higher-return assets like stocks, while those closer to retirement may prefer safer, income-generating investments.

3. **Research and Due Diligence:** Understanding the factors that influence the risk and return characteristics of different investments can inform better decision-making. Regular monitoring and assessment of investment performance against benchmarks and goals are crucial.

4. **Risk Management Techniques:** Using stop-loss orders, options, and other financial instruments can help investors manage risk and protect against significant losses.

5. **Consulting with Financial Professionals:** For many investors, seeking advice from financial advisors can provide tailored strategies that align with personal risk tolerances and financial objectives.

## Conclusion:

Balancing risk and returns is not about eliminating risk but rather about understanding and managing it to achieve desired financial outcomes. By carefully considering how much risk to take on in pursuit of investment returns, individuals can construct a portfolio that aligns with their goals, time horizon, and risk tolerance, setting the stage for financial growth and security.

# Chapter - 11

# The Hidden Opportunity in Pairing Health/Life Insurance with Mutual Funds

In the world of financial services, the ability to offer comprehensive solutions to clients is not just a value-add; it's a strategic necessity. When professionals in the sector overlook the potential of bundling health/life insurance with mutual funds, they miss out on a golden opportunity to enhance client satisfaction, deepen relationships, and drive growth. This book explores why integrating these products is crucial and how it can unlock significant benefits for both clients and advisors.

## Holistic Financial Planning

The essence of effective financial planning lies in its holistic approach. Clients seek not just to invest or insure but to secure their financial future comprehensively. Health and life insurance safeguard against unforeseen health crises and life's uncertainties, ensuring financial stability during difficult times. Mutual funds, on the other hand, offer the opportunity for wealth accumulation and financial growth. Together, they provide a balanced approach to financial planning, covering both protection and growth. By offering these products in tandem, advisors address a broader range of financial needs, which enhances client trust and satisfaction.

## Cross-Selling Efficiency

From a business perspective, the cross-selling of health/life insurance alongside mutual funds is an efficient strategy. It reduces the cost of client acquisition and increases the lifetime value of each client. When advisors present these bundled solutions, they demonstrate a comprehensive understanding of their clients' needs, which can significantly improve client retention rates. Moreover, satisfied clients are more likely to provide referrals, further reducing the cost and effort required for new client acquisition.

## Risk Management and Financial Stability

Integrating health/life insurance with investment products like mutual funds allows clients to manage their risks more effectively while pursuing their financial goals. Insurance provides a safety net that protects the client's financial plan against disruptions caused by health issues or life events. At the same time, mutual funds can be tailored to the client's risk tolerance and financial objectives, offering a diversified investment portfolio. This combination ensures that clients are not only protected against risks but are also positioned to achieve their long-term financial aspirations.

## Education and Engagement

By selling these products together, advisors have a unique opportunity to educate clients about the importance of both insurance and investment in financial planning. This educational process fosters deeper engagement, as clients learn to view their financial advisor as a trusted partner in their financial journey. Advisors who take the time to explain the synergies between protection and investment products can demystify financial planning, making it more accessible and engaging for their clients.

## Conclusion:

The integration of health/life insurance with mutual funds is more than just a sales strategy; it's a comprehensive approach to financial planning that benefits both clients and advisors. It offers a well-rounded solution that addresses immediate protection needs while setting the foundation for future financial growth. Advisors who leverage this approach can enhance their service offering, strengthen client relationships, and position themselves as indispensable partners in their clients' financial well-being. In an increasingly competitive financial services landscape, the ability to offer bundled, holistic solutions is not merely an advantage—it's imperative.

# Chapter - 12

# Strategies for Effective Selling in Financial Services

## Strategy for Selling Mutual Funds and Life/Health Insurance

To effectively sell both mutual funds and life/health insurance, a holistic approach to understanding client needs is essential. Financial advisors should:

## Conduct a Comprehensive Needs Analysis:

Understand the client's financial goals, risk tolerance, and investment horizon to tailor a strategy that incorporates both mutual funds and life/health insurance.

## Educate Clients:

 Many clients may not fully grasp how mutual funds and life/health insurance complement each other. Education on the benefits and purposes of each can empower clients to make informed decisions.

## Offer Customized Solutions:

Use the flexibility of mutual funds combined with the security of life/health insurance to create personalized financial plans that address specific client needs and goals.

## Highlight the Synergy:

Explain how mutual funds and life/health insurance work together to provide financial growth and protection, emphasizing the value of having a diversified and comprehensive financial portfolio.

In conclusion, mutual funds and life/health insurance are not just individual products but integral components of a holistic financial strategy. By offering these products, financial advisors can provide their clients with a balanced approach to achieving their financial objectives, ensuring both the protection and growth of their assets. This strategy not only benefits clients by offering them a comprehensive financial solution but also enhances the value provided by financial advisors, setting the foundation for long-term client relationships.

# Chapter - 13

# A Road Map to Follow

Successfully selling a comprehensive financial package, including high-value insurance and mutual fund investments, to a potential client requires a differential approach. Life and health insurance products serve as safeguards, managing risks associated with health and life, while mutual funds offer a pathway to wealth accumulation. It is essential to provide a holistic financial solution to your prospects, particularly to high-net-worth individuals (HNIs) who are often challenging to engage. The potential for wealth generation by leveraging this opportunity is significant. However, the journey to achieving such an ambitious goal is fraught with challenges.

1. The primary step towards selling these varied financial products effectively is ensuring you possess an in-depth understanding of mutual funds, life insurance, and health insurance. If you find gaps in your knowledge in any of these areas, it's prudent to collaborate with colleagues who are more knowledgeable. This partnership not only enriches your

understanding but also enhances your ability to offer comprehensive solutions to your clients.

2. Furthermore, it's vital to continually update your knowledge base and surround yourself with peers and mentors who inspire growth and improvement. This environment of continuous learning and mutual support is crucial for staying ahead in the competitive and ever-evolving financial services landscape.

3. Adopt a flexible and open-minded approach when engaging with clients. For instance, if a client expresses interest in purchasing life insurance products, seize the opportunity to broaden the conversation to include health insurance and mutual funds. This strategy not only demonstrates your comprehensive understanding of financial solutions but also highlights the benefits of a diversified investment portfolio. By effectively communicating the interconnectedness of these products and how they can collectively secure and enhance the client's financial health, you can cater to a broader range of their financial needs and aspirations.

4. Mastering the art of fact-finding is crucial in the financial advisory field. This process involves a detailed exploration and understanding of your client's current financial situation, goals, and risk tolerance. It's about asking the right questions to uncover not just the obvious financial needs but also those that

are less apparent. By doing so, you can tailor your recommendations to fit perfectly with the client's long-term objectives and immediate needs.

# Chapter – 14

# Fact-Finding: A Fundamental Requirement

Effective fact-finding requires active listening, empathy, and the ability to read between the lines. It's not just about filling out a questionnaire; it's about engaging in a meaningful conversation that helps build trust and rapport with your client. This approach enables you to identify opportunities where different financial products, such as mutual funds, life, and health insurance, can offer comprehensive solutions. By becoming proficient in fact-finding, you position yourself as a trusted advisor who can navigate your clients through their financial journey with confidence and expertise.

By meeting these prerequisites, you position yourself to successfully sell a diverse range of financial products to discerning prospects, maximizing their investment potential while securing their financial well-being.

# Chapter - 15

# A Real-Life Story of Selling Insurance and Mutual Funds continues....

## My Initial Meeting with a High-Net-Worth Client

Securing a meeting with a high-net-worth individual (HNI) was made seamless thanks to a strong referral, setting the stage for what would become a pivotal encounter in understanding and catering to his financial security needs, particularly in acquiring a Term Plan.

Here's how the events unfolded:

Upon arriving at his office five minutes before our scheduled meeting—a practice I adhere to out of professionalism and courtesy—I was greeted by the sight of a spacious and elegantly furnished office. My habit of making a pre-appointment confirmation call had once again proved its worth, ensuring our meeting commenced without delay.

The reception area, adorned with tasteful furniture and art, gave way to a conference hall where I was asked to wait momentarily. The personal secretary, having been notified of my arrival, played a crucial role in this smooth transition.

Shortly, Mr. Ramesh Patel made his entrance. His youthful and poised appearance, coupled with a smart casual attire, provided a warm and inviting start to our meeting. I took the chance to compliment him, playfully suggesting he could have a career in the film industry. His response was a good-natured laugh followed by a warm handshake. I often use these light-hearted icebreakers when meeting new people, and they consistently yield positive outcomes.

The atmosphere was perfectly primed for a meaningful conversation.

After a brief personal introduction and an overview of my work, I sought his permission to delve deeper into his needs through a series of questions, aimed at crafting a tailored solution for him.

Our conversation covered the following key questions:

## 1. The Motivation Behind Seeking Term Insurance:

Mr. Patel expressed a desire to ensure his family's financial security in his absence, highlighting the protective essence of the term insurance.

## 2. Major Concerns:

He voiced concerns over the implications for his business and the securities and personal guarantees offered to banks, in the event of his untimely demise and the potential inability of his company to repay loans.

## 3. Preferences for Term Insurance:

 Mr. Patel specified a preference for an affordable Term plan with a limited premium payment duration, extending up to the age of 80, emphasizing a desire for both coverage longevity and manageable costs.

Further discussions aimed to delve into the health of his business, the associated risks, and his personal financial landscape, both active and passive, to fully understand and address his financial aspirations and security.

This initial encounter marked the beginning of a thorough exploration into customizing financial products that aligned with Mr. Patel's unique needs, setting the foundation for a comprehensive financial security plan.

Here are the main issues and recommendations identified from our findings:

1.    **Secured Loans:**

      Mr. Ramesh Patel has secured loans totaling Rs. 50 Crores, backed by 200% collateral and personal guarantees. This situation is a significant concern as it shows the company's heavy reliance on Mr. Patel. He has pledged all his assets, including personal guarantees, which could pose a considerable risk to his successors in the event of his unforeseen departure.

      We also shared with him an article we authored, which details the critical aspects of personal guarantees.

# What happens to a Personal Guarantee if you die?

A personal guarantee is a promise to pay someone a debt that is owed by somebody else. Usually a personal guarantee is only called upon if the person who owes the money doesn't pay it when they have to.

## The Effect of Death

**A personal guarantee will usually last as long as the associated debt is outstanding. If you die while the personal guarantee is still alive, what does that mean for your estate?**

In a nutshell, usually, and subject to the terms of the document, **the guarantee does not die with your death. Instead, your estate continues to be liable under your personal guarantee. Can you imagine the consequences of that!**

**Here are just a few:**

1. Your estate cannot be finalised until the personal guarantee ends ie when the related debt is paid

2. If the debtor defaults in paying the debt, your estate will be called upon under the guarantee to meet the debt.

3. If the guarantee was given for the benefit of one of your children, the other children who are beneficiaries of your estate will not be pleased to say the least particularly if the guarantee is called upon and as a consequence, they lose some or all of their entitlements.

**What to do?**

Here are some options:

1. As always, one of your options is to do nothing and leave the guarantee in place and hope like hell that it won't come home to haunt you and your beneficiaries.

2. See your lawyer about the effect of your death on the terms of your particular personal guarantee and how you might adjust your Will to take into account the possibility of the guarantee falling on your estate's shoulders.

3. Explore the possibility of getting personal guarantee insurance to protect you or your estate if the guarantee is called upon.

4. See if you can get out of the guarantee which is usually extremely difficult unless some other form of security is offered to replace it.

We highlighted this risk to Mr. Patel and advised him to hedge all his Secured Liabilities worth Rs. 50 Crores, including personal guarantees. This strategy could mitigate major financial risks. Additionally, given his current insurance coverage, we advised acquiring an affordable Keyman Insurance Plan with a coverage amount of Rs. 50 Crores, effective only until he reaches the age of 60. By that time, he will have cleared all secured liabilities and personal guarantees associated with the business, making it unnecessary to continue the Keyman plan beyond that point.

## 2.    Health Insurance:

Currently, Mr. Patel's health insurance coverage is only Rs.5 Lakhs, which is insufficient given his lifestyle and the stress associated with his business. We suggested that he should obtain a comprehensive family Super Top-up health plan with a coverage of Rs.1 Crore and deductible of Rs. 5.00 Lacs to adequately protect against potential health issues.

### 3. Investments:

Suggesting an investment plan to someone primarily interested in a low-cost Protection Term plan can be challenging. Convincing a successful business owner to consider mutual funds over long-trusted investment avenues requires skilful communication. Our first step was to analyse his investment patterns and assess the Returns vs. Risks associated with his methods. Our findings indicated that Mr. Patel's investments were heavily concentrated in land and real estate, presenting a high-risk asset concentration strategy. To facilitate our discussion and build trust, we proposed the following questions:

Mr. Patel, are you aware of the following?

**1).  25 equity mutual fund schemes in India completed 25 years; offer around 17% average returns**

You can see, most of these funds managed to offer more than 12% returns in the last 25 years.

Source: ET Times, July 20, 2022

**2).**

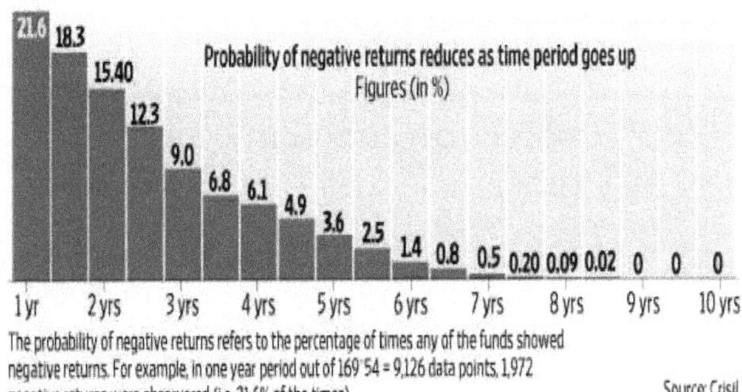


According to the long-term data shown in the Probability Chart of Negative Returns, investments held in Mutual Funds for more than six years almost eliminate the risk of capital loss.

**3). Not investing in equity could be the riskiest thing for an investor,** including retirees. Here are a few reasons why avoiding equity investments might be risky:

**a. Inflation Risk:** Equities are known for their potential to offer returns that can outpace inflation over the long term. By not investing in equities, one may find that his savings lose purchasing power over time as inflation diminishes the real value of money held in fixed-income or other lower-yielding investments.

**b. Opportunity Cost:** Equity markets, especially in a growing economy like India, offer substantial growth opportunities. Over the past decades, Indian equities have delivered substantial returns, reflecting the country's economic growth. Investors who avoid equities miss out on these gains, which can compound significantly over time.

**c. Diversification:** Equity investments provide an essential diversification benefit. By investing only in fixed income or other asset classes like real estate, investors risk higher exposure to specific economic or market downturns affecting those sectors. Equities often perform differently under various economic conditions, providing a balance that can reduce overall portfolio risk.

**d. Longevity Risk:** With increasing life expectancy, retirees need their savings to last longer. Equities provide potential for growth, which is crucial for funding a longer retirement. Without the growth from equities, there's a higher risk of depleting retirement funds prematurely.

**e. Reduced Income Flow:** Fixed-income investments typically provide regular income, but these might not be sufficient to meet all financial needs, especially as costs rise over time. Equities can offer dividends in addition to capital gains, which can grow over the years and help maintain a comfortable lifestyle.

**f. Market Timing Risks:** By avoiding equities based on short-term market fluctuations or past downturns, investors may miss the ideal times to enter the market which can result in long-term growth opportunities. Historically, those who remain invested over longer periods tend to experience fewer negative effects from volatility and enjoy substantial returns.

By understanding these risks, even retired individuals can appreciate the potential benefits of maintaining a balanced portfolio that includes equities, tailored of course to their specific risk tolerance and financial goals.

## 4). Investment in Mutual funds are tax savy.

Investing in mutual funds can be tax-efficient in
several ways, particularly in India. Here are some of
the key tax advantages:

### a. Equity-Linked Savings Scheme (ELSS):

Investments in ELSS mutual funds qualify for tax
deductions under Section 80C of the Income Tax Act.
This section allows for a deduction of up to ₹1.5 lakh
per financial year from taxable income. ELSS funds
have a lock-in period of three years, which is shorter
than other tax-saving instruments like Public
Provident Fund (PPF) or National Savings Certificates
(NSC).

### b. Long-Term Capital Gains (LTCG) Tax:

For equity mutual funds, Long-Term Capital Gains
over ₹1 lakh are taxed at 12.5% without indexation
benefit if the investment is held for more than one
year. This is comparatively lower than the tax rates on
interest income from fixed deposits.

### c. Dividend Distribution Tax (DDT):

As of the 2020 financial year, dividends paid by
mutual funds are taxable in the hands of the investors
at their applicable income tax rate. While this is a tax,
it does allow for managing tax liabilities better,
especially for investors in lower tax brackets.

### d. Systematic Withdrawal Plan (SWP):

SWPs can be used as a tax-efficient way to create a
regular income stream. In SWPs, only the gains
portion of each withdrawal is taxed, which can
potentially lower the tax liability compared to
receiving interest income.

These features make mutual funds an attractive option for those looking to minimize their tax liability while potentially enhancing their returns. It's advisable to consult with a tax advisor or financial planner to better understand the specific impacts based on individual financial situations.

Following our conversation, it became clear that diversifying his investment portfolio through initiating a Systematic Investment Plan (SIP) of Rs. 2 Lakhs per month into a low-risk balanced advantage fund was a sensible recommendation. This strategy aims to spread risk and potentially secure stable returns, net of taxes, over time. Additionally, it ensures that there is adequate liquidity available as needed.

**Conclusion:**

The engagement with Mr. Ramesh Patel underscores the critical role of personalized financial planning, especially for high-net-worth individuals facing complex financial landscapes. Through detailed consultations, we identified key areas of concern such as the impact of personal guarantees on his estate, underinsurance in both life and health sectors, and a heavily concentrated investment in real estate. By addressing these issues, we not only catered to his immediate needs but also set a strategic path for future financial stability and growth.

Our recommendations for securing additional insurance coverage and diversifying his investment portfolio through mutual funds are aimed at mitigating risks and maximizing returns. These steps are crucial in ensuring that Mr. Patel's financial setup is resilient against unforeseen circumstances, thereby safeguarding his family's welfare and his business interests. By initiating a systematic investment plan and considering tax-efficient mutual funds, we provide a balanced approach to achieving both short-term liquidity and long-term financial security.

This case illustrates the importance of a comprehensive approach in financial planning, where understanding the client's unique situation leads to tailored solutions that address both immediate concerns and future aspirations. As financial advisors, our goal remains to empower our clients through informed decisions and strategic planning, ensuring their peace of mind and financial security for years to come.

# Chapter - 16

## Connect with fellow travellers for richer experience. -  A real life story - 2

You might find this tale intriguing. It's about how I managed to sell a high-value mutual fund along with a term and health insurance plan to a fellow traveller during my vacation to Australia and New Zealand.

Every year, as part of my holiday routine, I embark on a journey to explore new destinations for about 10 to 20 days. This particular year, I chose Australia and New Zealand for a 20-day adventure. I prefer traveling solo but joining group tours, which offers a fantastic opportunity to meet and engage with new people. Naturally sociable, I enjoy striking conversations with strangers, turning many into friends globally. Merging with new groups comes easily to me, and our exchanges range from business and politics to health, among other topics. Directly selling my products isn't my go-to approach.

Yet, curiosity arises when they learn about my multifaceted role as an author, speaker, and financial product advisor. My brief self-introduction, lasting about 30 seconds, often piques their interest further, making them keen to discover how I might assist them. This brief interaction often leads to discussions about financial products.

**30 seconds Self introduction**

*"My name is Randhir.*

*Randhir Bhalla*

*We are the Risks Managers.*

*We help manage Critical Risks in your life and Business to make certain that you will never be poor.*

*Our job is to protect and create wealth.*

*Take a minute to check out our organization details*

*==> https://youtu.be/QQtdF8rWgnE"*

To give you a clearer picture, let me share a specific instance that illustrates how smoothly I was able to sell comprehensive financial solutions, including mutual funds, life insurance, and health insurance, in one go.

On the first day of our bus journey, we were prompted to introduce ourselves. During this session, I met Mr. Prakash Soni, a 42-year-old Gujarati IT Professional traveling with his wife, Urvashi, who is a year or two youngers than him and 2 children. Mr. Prakash quickly showed an interest in my services, eager to understand how I could assist in growing and safeguarding his wealth.

Initially, I hesitated, as I typically prefer to keep my vacation separate from business. Nonetheless, Mr. Prakash persisted, and we agreed to meet later at the hotel's coffee shop to discuss further.

Continue reading in the next chapter...

# Chapter - 17

## A Memorable Evening Unfolds: The Story Continues...

That evening, as planned, we sat down together.

Mr. Prakash was evidently eager and somewhat impatient, anticipating some immediate, impactful advice from me. Before diving into potential solutions, I knew I needed to gather comprehensive information about his financial situation and goals.

Here's a detailed record of the facts I gathered about Mr. Prakash Soni during our meeting:

Facts Finding

Name – Mr. Prakash Soni

Age – 40

Occupation – Software Engineer

Residence – Andheri West

Income (Annual Salary) – Rs. 60.00 Lacs

Health - Good

Habits- No smoking/ Alcohol - Social Drinker

Previous insurance – Rs. 1 Cr Term Plan

Liabilities (Home Loan) – 2.00 Crs.

Investments – Owned a flat worth Rs. 4.00 Crs. where he is residing at present.

Aware of virtue of investing in mutual funds. However, not made significant investments so far.

Family Members – Wife- Homemaker

Parents supported by him.

Son – 8 Yrs,                 Daughter – 12 yrs.

Health Plan – Rs. 10.00 Lacs provided by the Co.

Keen to purchase a suitable Term Plan

Gathering income-based documents can be challenging, but I was able to collect a substantial amount of information through straightforward conversations. This data is now sufficient to devise a detailed plan aimed at protecting and enhancing my client's wealth.

**Principles I adhere to when crafting an irresistible offer.**

1. **Protection Over Returns:** The primary concern of a financial advisor should be the client's protection. This includes ensuring they have comprehensive health coverage and a robust protection plan. Only once these foundations are secure do I consider wealth creation strategies.

2. **Multiple Options:** I always present two tailored solutions, giving clients the freedom to choose the one that suits them best. This approach not only demonstrates thorough consideration and effort but also resonates well with clients, as they feel actively involved in the decision-making process.

### 3. Professional Presentation:

Taking a cue from the iconic James Bond, I dress sharply and communicate gently. I often introduce myself with the classic line, "My name is Bond. James Bond," accompanied by a warm handshake. This not only lightens the mood but also sets a positive tone for the discussions that follow.

### 4. Comprehensive and Innovative Solutions:

My strategies are designed to be comprehensive and innovative, ensuring they stand out from those offered by competitors. This approach involves thinking outside the box to provide solutions that truly meet the unique needs of each client.

**How to differentiate and prepare an Irresistible Offer.**

**Follow 2 rules.**

In creating/ presenting customized financial solutions, I adhere to several key principles:

By following these guidelines, I ensure that my services not only meet but exceed the expectations of my clients, fostering a productive and trust-filled advisor-client relationship.

## RULE NO. 1

**Dress Nice
Speak Gentle with Manners
Just like the Bonds**

## RULE NO. 2

### Always provide 2 Options

### Why?

Because it.... Builds Trust: By presenting two options, it shows that you've considered multiple solutions for the buyer, indicating that you're more interested in meeting their needs than pushing a single agenda.

### A Gateway to HNI's Life

### Option -1

Build Your Legacy,

Live Without Fear.

A term plan that provides coverage up to the age of 80 with a limited premium payment term.

| Sum Assured | Term | Premium with GST ( Yearly ) | Total Premium In Lacs |
|---|---|---|---|
| 10 Cr. | 40 Years Pay for 30 Yrs IRR 6.29% on death at age 80. Guaranteed Tax free | 6,15,558 | 185 |

Educate the client prior to introducing Option-2.

## A). India Life Expectancy 1950-2023

| Year | Life Expectancy |
|---|---|
| 2023 | 70.42 |
| 2022 | 70.19 |
| 2021 | 69.96 |

## B). A Few Alarming Facts of the Life

- Mumbaikars die younger than other Indians: Study | India News
- Delhi has been declared the world's most polluted city.
- The average lifespan of Delhi residents is expected to
- by 11.9 years.
  - A recent WHO Report

## C). What are the objectives of buying a Term Plan?

- To hedge the liabilities / personal guarantees.

- To replace the income in case of death.

## D). When is a person not required to have any insurance coverage?

If the prospect has no liabilities / personal gurantees and sufficient passive income to sustain their lifestyle even in their permanent absence, there is no need for a Term Plan.

## E). Central questions to consider are:

1. Why would one need the same level of insurance coverage when liabilities are decreasing, and personal net worth is on the rise?

2. Is there a need for insurance up to the age of 80, even when there are no outstanding liabilities or income to substitute?

**F). Your Offer should be Irresistible.**

Maximizing value for every penny invested.

**Option -2 An Irresistible Offer**

After educating the prospects on the fundamental principles of protection and investments, it is now appropriate to present Solution Option 2.

Based on the information provided, here is an irresistible offer that I have prepared and presented to my client.

- A Pure Term Plan – Up to Rs. 15.00 Crs (Tax Free)

- Premium / Investment – Up to Rs. 6.15 Lacs P. A. (Less than 0.41 % of the Sum Assured)

- Total Investment – Rs. 153.75.00 Lacs

- Amount available at Age 65 – Rs. 3.24 Crs. (Based on Track Record)

- Liquidity when you want.

- You can terminate the plan early without any penalties on surrender.

- Health Insurance for Family Rs. 50. 00 Lacs

# A Plan Combination

| Sum Assured | Term | Premium | Total Premium | Protection Available upto the Age |
|---|---|---|---|---|
| | | with GST (Yearly) | in lacs | |
| 2.5 Cr. | 10 | 53,368 | 5,33,680 | 50 – 15 Crs. |
| 5 Cr | 15 | 1,25,381 | 18,80,715 | 55 – 12.5 Crs. |
| 5 Cr. | 20 | 1,50,084 | 30,01,680 | 60 - 7.5 Crs |
| 2.5 Cr. | 25 | 88,093 | 22,02,325 | 65 – 2.5 Crs. |
| Total = 15 Cr. | | 4,16,926 | 76,18,400 | |

**Your Goal Is Every penny invested creates a value.**

## A Value Creation Chart

| Future Value of Rs. 53368 at 12% for 15 years | 41.75 x 53368 | = | 2228114 |
|---|---|---|---|
| Future Value of Rs. 125381 for 12% for 10 years | 19.65 x 125381 | = | 2463736.65 |
| Future value of Rs. 150084 for 12% for 5 years | 7.12 x 150084 | = | 1068598.08 |
| Total Earnings on Maturity | | = | 5760448.73 |
| Future Value of Rs. 1.78 Lacs @ 12 % for 25 years | 149.30x178000 | = | 26575400.00 |
| Total Earnings on Maturity | | = | 32335848.73 |
| | Say | | 3.24 Crs |

A discerning observer of the recommended plan will see that it integrates three distinct offers:

1. A Term Plan for a sum up to Rs. 15.00 Cr.

2. A Super Top-Up Health Plan with Rs. 3.00 Lacs deductible covering Rs. 50.00 Lacs.

3. A Mutual Fund SIP projected to accumulate Rs. 3.24 Cr. (based on the historical performance of the fund) by the age of 65.

## Can you outdo this uniquely designed comprehensive Financial Plan?

## The Concluding Part of the Story

The final segment of the story is up to your imagination. Let me know your thoughts on how it ends and receive a discount coupon for my next training session.

# Prepare to elevate your skills and reach new heights with our comprehensive program.

## Our Ultimate Sales Skills (USS) Training Programs

In this book, you've merely glimpsed a single droplet, but there is an entire ocean waiting for you to explore. Immerse yourself in our Ultimate Sales Skills (USS) Training Programs to dive deeper into this world.

What can you expect to gain from this program?

Our program primarily emphasizes innovation, aiming to inspire the transformations you desire. We'll equip you with exclusive tools and techniques taught at the world's leading business schools.

Drawing from my extensive 45-year corporate journey, I will share invaluable knowledge and insights to help you grow.

Prepare to elevate your skills and reach new heights with our comprehensive program.

# Transformational Testimonials

In this section, we present heartfelt testimonials from individuals who have experienced significant transformations through our training. Their words reflect the profound impact and practical value of the lessons they have learned. These testimonials serve as a testament to the effectiveness of our approach and the tangible benefits it brings to their professional and personal lives.

Here are some of their inspiring stories:

Tul Bahadur – New Delhi

"Sir, what you have taught is profound and reflects real-world scenarios. I am committed to understanding it because it is a valuable treasure. Implementing even 75% of it can lead to astonishing growth. No one else teaches this way, addressing actual challenges. Salute to you."

Sunil Gaikwad, Mumbai

"It has been an incredible experience. We are confident that we will benefit greatly from your training in the future. Thank you so much, sir 🙏."

Neel Kamal Sood, New Delhi

"This training course is different from all other courses, sir. I will definitely implement the ideas."

M. Raja, Vishakapatnam

"According to me, instead of being life-changing, this session is life-giving to us 🙏."

Swarup Jena, Sundargarh

"I am from Sundargarh, Odisha. Before, I mentioned that I closed 32 lakhs in regular premium after reading two books."

Prakash, Cochin

"Your sessions are very powerful. We now understand the dignity of our profession. Thank you so much, sir."

Ashok Bhowmick, Kolkata

"USS6 is the most unique workshop I have ever attended. Now I can select my prospects and understand what HNIs want, providing irresistible offers based on their needs. Needless to say, I am now confident in introducing myself. I am Ashok Bhowmick, a Risk Manager."

These testimonials highlight the diverse ways in which our training has empowered individuals, enabling them to achieve new heights in their professional journeys.

# We eagerly await your review of this book.

During our 14 training sessions, the Author emphasize the importance of carving a niche in the financial sector by doing what others cannot, a fundamental strategy for achieving financial independence and a luxurious lifestyle in retirement.

Please share your thoughts and comments by writing a review.